GEO

The Continents

by Jennifer Waters

Content and Reading Adviser: Mary Beth Fletcher, Ed.D.
Educational Consultant/Reading Specialist
The Carroll School, Lincoln, Massachusetts

COMPASS POINT BOOKS

Minneapolis, Minnesota

Compass Point Books
3722 West 50th Street, #115
Minneapolis, MN 55410

Visit Compass Point Books on the Internet at *www.compasspointbooks.com*
or e-mail your request to *custserv@compasspointbooks.com*

Photographs ©: Rubberball Productions, cover (girl); PhotoDisc, 4, 5, 6, 8, 12, 17; Comstock, Inc., 7; TRIP/C. Hamilton, 9; TRIP/B. Gadsby, 10; TRIP/M. Thornton, 11; TRIP/P. Rauter, 13; Corel, 14; Ann Ronan Picture Library, 15; TRIP/J. Pugh, 16; TRIP/E. Smith, 18, 19.

Project Manager: Rebecca Weber McEwen
Editor: Heidi Schoof
Photo Researcher: Image Select International Limited
Photo Selectors: Rebecca Weber McEwen and Heidi Schoof
Designer: Jaime Martens
Illustrator: Anna-Maria Crum

Library of Congress Cataloging-in-Publication Data

Waters, Jennifer.
 The continents / by Jennifer Waters.
     p. cm. — (Spyglass books)
Summary: Briefly introduces Earth's seven continents: Europe, Asia, Africa, North America, South America, Australia, and Antarctica. Includes bibliographical references (p. 23) and index.
 ISBN 0-7565-0378-7 (hardcover)
 1. Continents—Juvenile literature. [1. Continents.] I. Title.
 II. Series.
 G133 .W38 2002
 910'.914'1—dc21

                    2002002557

Contents

Where on Earth?

If you are on Earth, you are either in water or on land.
Earth's biggest land masses are called continents.

A.

B.

Seven Continents

A. North America

B. South America

C. Europe

D. Asia

E. Africa

F. Australia

G. Antarctica

C.

D.

E.

F.

G.

North America

North America reaches from just below the **North Pole** to just above the **equator**. North America has deserts, jungles, mountains, forests, and even **ice caps**.

The Rocky Mountains

The Grand Canyon

Did You Know?

The Grand Canyon is in North America. In some places it is 10 miles (16 kilometers) wide and 1 mile (1.6 kilometers) deep!

South America

South America sits south of North America. Mountains run along its west coast. The top part of the continent is *rain forest.* To the south, there are *grasslands.*

Machu Picchu

The Atacama Desert

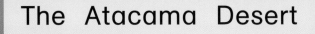

Did You Know?

South America has the driest place on Earth. In the Atacama Desert, it rains once or twice every 100 years.

Europe

Europe is a small continent that is above the equator. Europe has many mountains. Many people live and work in Europe's flat areas of land.

Pyrenees mountains

A cave

Did You Know?
France is a country in Europe. It has many big caves in its mountains.

Africa

Africa is Earth's second-largest continent. The middle of Africa is a warm, wet forest. Around the forest are grasslands and deserts.

African grasslands

The Nile

Did You Know?

The world's longest river is in Africa.

It is called the Nile.

Australia

Australia is the world's smallest continent and the world's largest island. The middle of Australia is mostly desert. Australia also has rain forests and mountains.

Australian outback

Uluru

Did You Know?
The world's largest rock is in Australia. Some people call it Uluru. Others call it Ayers Rock.

Antarctica

Antarctica is at the very south tip of Earth. The **South Pole** sits right in the middle of it. Antarctica is the coldest place on Earth.

Antarctic ice caps

Did You Know?

Ice is heavy. Scientists think that if Antarctica's ice melted, the land underneath it would rise about 2,000 feet (610 meters)!

The Super Continent

Millions of years ago, all of Earth's land was one huge continent.
This piece of land slowly broke apart into our seven continents.

This large mass of land was called Pangaea.

The continents are still moving. This movement is so slow, you can't feel it.

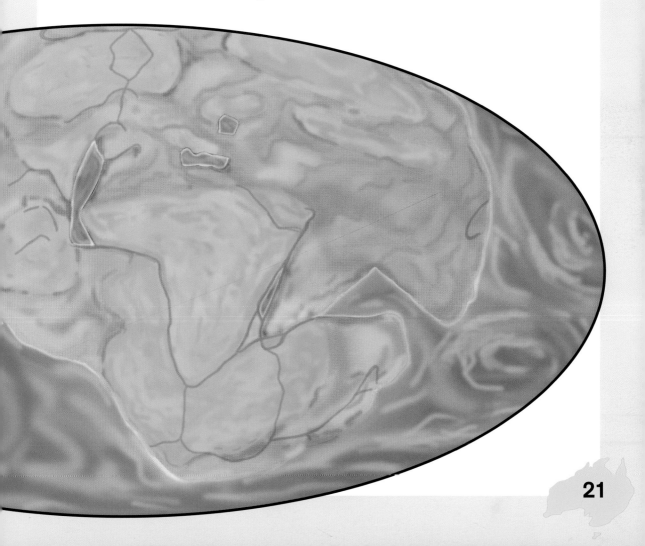

Glossary

equator–an imaginary line around
the middle of Earth

grassland–land where the main plants
are grasses

ice cap–land that is always covered in
ice and snow

North Pole–the part of Earth that is
the farthest north

plain–a big area of land where
there are no trees

rain forest–a kind of forest where more
than 100 inches (254 cm) of rain falls
every year

South Pole–the part of Earth that is
the farthest south

Learn More

Books

Beginner's World Atlas. Washington, D.C.: National Geographic Society, 1999.

First Picture Atlas. New York: Kingfisher, 1994.

Platt, Richard. *Explorers: Pioneers Who Broke New Boundaries.* New York: Dorling Kindersley, 2001.

Web Sites

visibleearth.nasa.gov

yahooligans.com/content/ka/almanac/ world/index.html

Index

GR: I
Word Count: 233

From Jennifer Waters

I live near the Rocky Mountains,
but the ocean is my favorite place.
I like to write songs and books.
I hope you enjoyed this book.

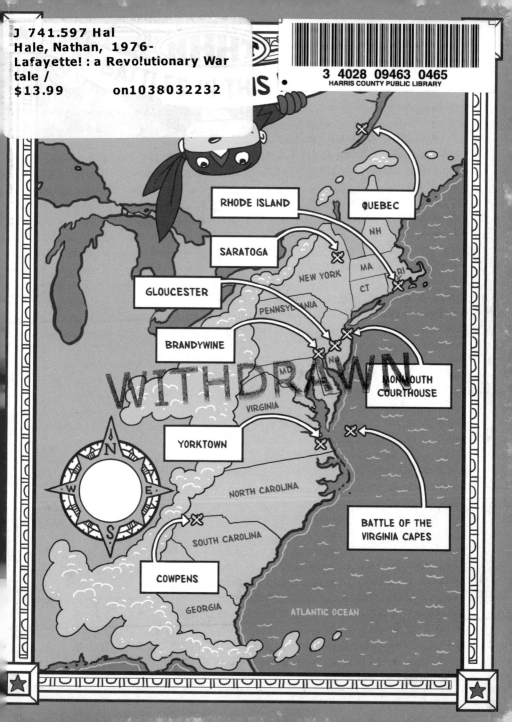

RHODE ISLAND

QUEBEC

NH

SARATOGA

NEW YORK

MA

CT

RI

GLOUCESTER

PENNSYLVANIA

BRANDYWINE

MD

MONMOUTH
COURTHOUSE

WITHDRAWN

VIRGINIA

YORKTOWN

N

W   E

S

NORTH CAROLINA

BATTLE OF THE
VIRGINIA CAPES

SOUTH CAROLINA

COWPENS

GEORGIA

ATLANTIC OCEAN

AMULET BOOKS, NEW YORK

CATALOGING--IN--PUBLICATION DATA HAS BEEN APPLIED FOR AND MAY BE OBTAINED FROM THE LIBRARY OF CONGRESS.
ISBN 978--1--4197--3148--8

TEXT AND ILLUSTRATIONS COPYRIGHT © 2018 NATHAN HALE
BOOK DESIGN BY NATHAN HALE AND CHAD W. BECKERMAN

PRINTED AND BOUND IN CHINA
10 9 8 7 6 5 4 3 2 1

AMULET BOOKS ARE AVAILABLE AT SPECIAL DISCOUNTS WHEN PURCHASED IN QUANTITY FOR PREMIUMS AND PROMOTIONS AS WELL AS FUNDRAISING OR EDUCATIONAL USE. SPECIAL EDITIONS CAN ALSO BE CREATED TO SPECIFICATION. FOR DETAILS, CONTACT SPECIALSALES@ABRAMSBOOKS.COM OR THE ADDRESS BELOW.

ABRAMS The Art of Books
195 Broadway, New York, NY 10007
abramsbooks.com